Rhode Island

Ocean Sites & City Lights : A Collection of Photographs

Stephanie Izzo

SUNLIGHT, MOONLIGHT, FIRELIGHT, NEON LIGHT.
DIRECTED, REFLECTED, REFRACTED, FILTERED. IN NATURE'S LANDSCAPES OR ON MAN'S CITYSCAPES.

NO MATTER THEIR SOURCE OR QUALITY OR RESTING PLACE, THE LIGHTS THAT SHINE ON RHODE ISLAND'S NARRAGANSETT BAY AND ON ITS CAPITAL CITY OF PROVIDENCE REVEAL MORE THAN SHAPES, COLORS, AND TEXTURES. THEY REVEAL SECRETS, STORIES, MEMORIES, AND SOULS. PROMISES, DREAMS, TRIALS, AND TRIUMPHS. AND A TIMELESS BEAUTY THAT IS TESTAMENT TO NATURE'S MAGNIFICENCE, MAN'S SPIRIT, AND THE INSPIRING COMBINATION OF THE TWO.

RHODE ISLAND IS KNOWN AS THE OCEAN STATE. WHILE IT MAY SEEM A BIT AUDACIOUS FOR THE SMALLEST STATE TO TAKE ITS NICKNAME FROM SOMETHING AS VAST AS THE ATLANTIC OCEAN, IT REFLECTS THE CHARMING BRAVADO THAT IS AN ESSENTIAL ELEMENT OF RHODE ISLAND'S INDOMITABLE CHARACTER. AND WITH 400 MILES OF COASTLINE IN A STATE THAT MEASURES ONLY 37 MILES WIDE BY 48 MILES LONG, IT'S NOT SURPRISING THAT AN INTENSELY INTIMATE RELATIONSHIP WOULD DEVELOP BETWEEN THE TINY STATE AND ITS MONUMENTAL NEIGHBOR.

FROM PROVIDENCE'S ARCHITECTURE, CITYSCAPES, AND URBAN VIGNETTES TO THE BAY'S BEACHES, LIGHTHOUSES, AND OTHER WATERFRONT TREASURES, THESE IMAGES OF LANDMARKS AND LOCALES BEAUTIFULLY CAPTURE A CITY AND A SEA THAT SHARE A UNIQUELY INTERTWINED HISTORY.

"As I gaze upon the sea!
All the old romantic legends,
all my dreams, come back to me."

~Henry Wadsworth Longfellow

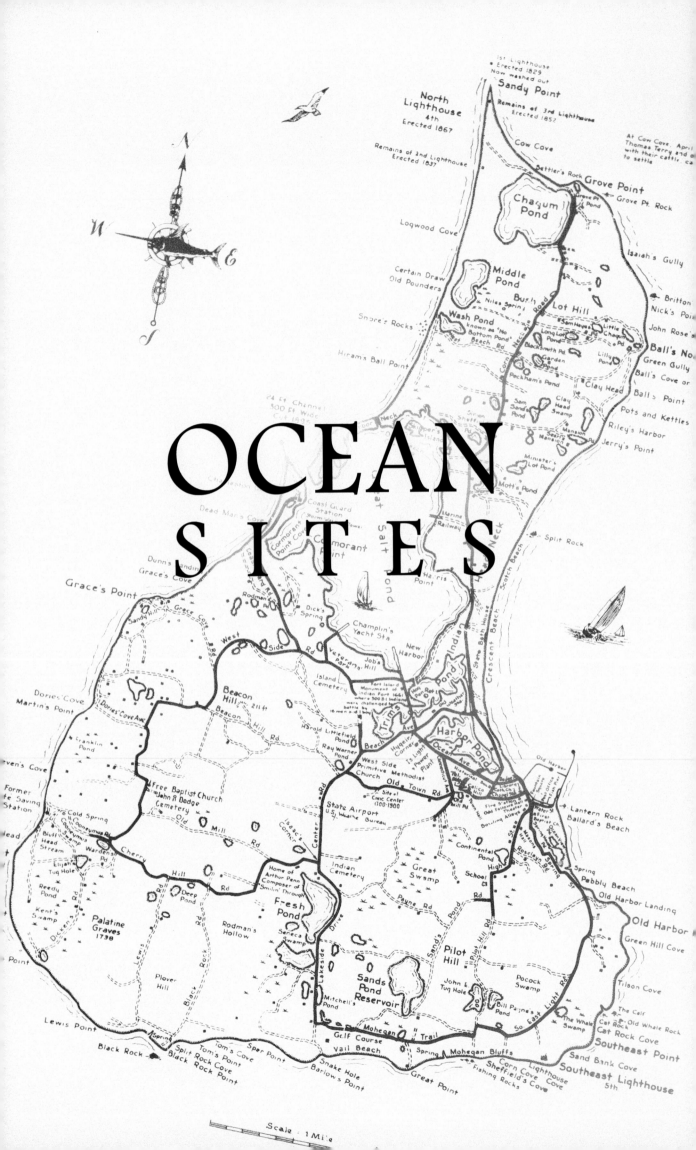

OCEAN
SITES

SUNSET OVER GOAT ISLAND

One of the most treasured historic icons of the city,
Goat Island Light has welcomed sailors into Newport Harbor since 1842.

HOPE
The Rhode Island State Motto

Wispy clouds drift through a powder-blue sky,

while the setting sun casts a copper glow on the stern of a boat moored at Bowen's Wharf in Newport.

AERIAL VIEW OF GOAT ISLAND

In past lives, it served as a colonial goat pasture, a nineteenth century fort, and a U.S. naval torpedo station. Today, the scenic retreat of Goat Island basks in its role as the base for world-class sailing regattas.

AERIAL VIEW OF ROSE ISLAND

Located just south of the Newport Bridge, Rose Island's Native American name was "Conockonoquit" ("place of the long point"). Used in the Revolutionary War and both World Wars for the defense of the Narragansett Bay, the tiny 18-acre island's rich and varied history earned it a listing on the National Register of Historic Places.

A BIRD'S EYE VIEW OF EASTON'S BEACH

Sunseekers find exactly what they're looking for along the warm sands of Easton's Beach in Newport.
More than 100 public and private beaches line Rhode Island's surprisingly lengthy 400+ mile coastline.

THE NEWPORT CLIFF WALK

Combining the scenic beauty of the Atlantic coast with the architectural grandeur of Newport's Gilded Age, the world-famous 3.5 mile Cliff Walk attracts hundreds of thousands of visitors every year:

NEWPORT HARBOR FROM 500 FT.

One of the finest harbors on the East Coast, Newport Harbor can host nearly 3,000 boats of all shapes and sizes on its busiest days. In addition to its rich maritime history, the harbor is also the exclusive home of the six legendary America's Cup yachts designed by the Herreshoffs of Bristol.

THE SCHOONER ADIRONDACK II
A Newport Mainstay since 1999

With her sleek lines, spacious 65' deck and just under 2,000 square feet of canvas,
an invigorating sail aboard this elegant turn-of-the-century-style schooner
is an unforgettable experience.

2(

SUNSET OVER NARRAGANSETT BAY

Calm seas stretch toward the Claiborne Pell Newport Bridge,
reflecting an Indian summer sunset as seen from the Goat Island causeway.

BEAVERTAIL LIGHT

Constructed in 1856 and situated on the southern point of Conanicut Island's rocky coastline, Beavertail Light remains a beloved and enduring symbol of Jamestown's early seafaring days.

SAINT MARY'S CHURCH

Established in 1828, St. Mary's Parish in Newport is the oldest Catholic parish in Rhode Island. Designated a National Historic Shrine, the beautiful second period Gothic style church was the location of Jacqueline Bouvier's wedding to John F. Kennedy in 1953.

DUSK AT CASTLE HILL LIGHT

Guarding the east entrance to Narragansett Bay,
Castle Hill Light marks the finish line for the biennial Annapolis to Newport sailboat race.

THE NEWPORT BRIDGE AT MIDNIGHT

The lights of the 11,248-foot long Claiborne Pell Newport Bridge shine in the nighttime mist like a string of sparkling diamonds.

APRIL SHOWERS OVER NEWPORT HARBOR

A handful of anchored sailboats bob against the painterly backdrop of clouds scudding across a rain-swept Narragansett Bay.

BLOCK ISLAND
BERMUDA OF THE NORTH

Named by Dutch explorer Adrian Block in 1614, the 11-square-mile rustic paradise of Block Island is home to an impressive 365 freshwater ponds, 32 miles of trails and 17 miles of pastel sand. Beckoning day-trippers with its Victorian charm and turquoise waters, the teardrop shaped island is a short 12-mile ferry ride off the coast of Rhode Island.

THE MOHEGAN BLUFFS AND SOUTHEAST LIGHT

Stretching nearly three miles along Block Island's pristine south side,
the 150-feet-high Mohegan Bluffs offer breathtaking views of the island's wind-swept coastline and the vast Atlantic Ocean.

BLOCK ISLAND SOUTHEAST LIGHT

*A symbol of maritime history and architectural ingenuity,
the 1875 Victorian-Gothic Southeast Light boasts one of the most powerful electric beacons
on the coast of the United States.*

BLOCK ISLAND NORTH LIGHT

Constructed in 1867, Block Island North Light represents the fourth attempt to establish a lighthouse on the shifting sands of Sandy Point.

More than a century later, the granite tower and surrounding dunes remain, preserved by the Block Island National Wildlife Refuge as an interpretive center and a seagull rookery.

THE OAR
Great Salt Pond

*Mouth-watering seafood and exquisite interior decor make the Oar
one of Block Island's signature seafood stops.*

*Sought out by visitors for its unrivaled view of the Boat Basin in New Harbor,
the restaurant is famous for the dizzying array of colorfully painted oars
that hang from its ceiling.*

WATCH HILL LIGHT AT DUSK

As daylight begins to fade, the blue waters of Little Narragansett Bay ripple and swirl around Watch Hill's sea-chiseled rocks. Nestled in Rhode Island's southwestern tip, this seaside village is home to one of the oldest lighthouse sites in the United States.

SUNSET AT WATCH HILL BEACH

Driven by childhood imagination (or perhaps the spirits of the Niantic Indians who once used this area as a lookout), a little boy stands at water's edge, surveying the horizon for incoming ships.

THE NARRAGANSETT TOWERS

One of America's best-known summer vacation destinations, Narragansett is located in Rhode Island's South County. The elegant towers, formerly part of the Narragansett Pier Casino, have withstood hurricanes and fires since 1886, faithfully remaining Narragansett's strongest link to the past.

POINT JUDITH LIGHT AT SUNSET

Located on the west side of the entrance to Narragansett Bay, the easily recognizable 51-foot octagonal tower of Point Judith Light was constructed in 1856. In 1871, the song of Point Judith was famously changed from horn to whistle, allowing its voice to be heard against the sirens of Beavertail Light.

THE MOUNT HOPE BRIDGE
FIRST BRIDGE OVER NARRAGANSETT BAY

Connecting the towns of Portsmouth and Bristol, the Mount Hope Bridge, built in 1929, proudly remained New England's longest suspension bridge for four decades — until the 1969 opening of the Claiborne Pell Newport Bridge.

EVENING SOLITUDE AT CHARLESTOWN BEACH

The tide rises as night falls, shrouding the soft white sands of Charlestown Beach in shades of purple.

THIS CITY NOW DOES, LIKE A GARMENT, WEAR
THE BEAUTY OF THE MORNING; SILENT, BARE,
SHIPS, TOWERS, DOMES, THEATRES, AND TEMPLES LIE
OPEN UNTO THE FIELDS, AND TO THE SKY;
ALL BRIGHT AND GLITTERING IN THE SMOKELESS AIR.

~WILLIAM WORDSWORTH

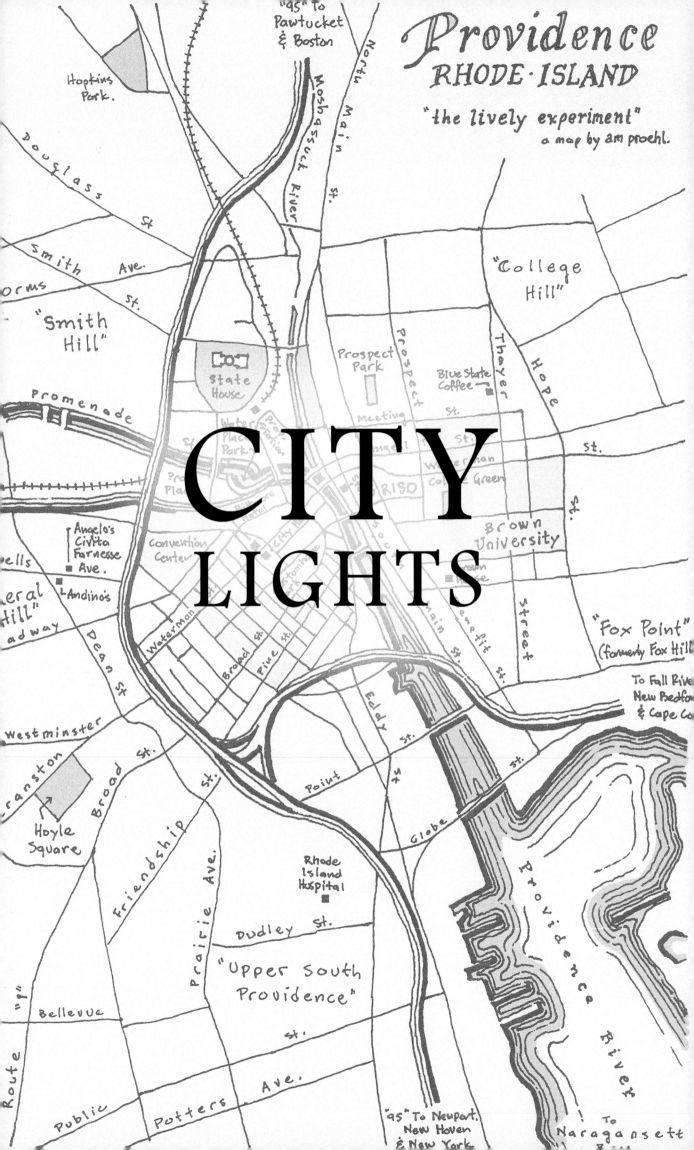

PROVIDENCE'S RIVERFRONT RENAISSANCE

For nearly 100 years, the Providence River remained hidden by a sea of asphalt,
often referred to as "the world's widest bridge."

After a dozen years of work and tens of millions of dollars,
the river (formed by the convergence of the Moshassuck and the Woonasquatucket Rivers)
was fully uncovered in 1996, reuniting the city with its lost waterfronts.

WATERFIRE REFLECTIONS

Since 1994, Barnaby Evans' magnificent WaterFire display has attracted between 10,000 to 100,000 visitors per lighting. The dazzling brilliance of the bonfires on the water, accompanied by the enchanting blend of world and classical music, makes this work of art one of the greatest symbols of Providence's ongoing renaissance.

WATERPLACE PARK

The 1994 completion of Waterplace Park and Riverwalk marks a crowning achievement in the revitalization of downtown Providence. Providing a four-acre venue for a variety of cultural events, the impeccable design of the park's cobblestone walkways and Venetian-style footbridges has earned national and international awards.

THE VIEW FROM PROSPECT PARK

Completed in 1939, this spectacular 14-foot granite statue was erected as a memorial for Roger Williams, the principal founder of Rhode Island. Williams is portrayed as standing on the bow of a canoe with his arm outstretched, blessing the city of Providence.

THE PROVIDENCE SKYLINE

The sun dips behind the few tall buildings of the city's compact skyline
as the warm glow of flickering lights begins to illuminate the Providence River.

INTERIOR VIEW OF THE RHODE ISLAND STATEHOUSE

The Rhode Island State House, completed in December 1900, is home to famous paintings and historical treasures, including the original colonial charter of 1663 from King Charles II. Its gleaming marble dome, modeled after the dome of St. Peter's Basilica, is the fourth-largest unsupported dome in the world.

VMA ARTS & CULTURAL CENTER AND RENAISSANCE HOTEL

Located at 1 Avenue of the Arts, the opulent 1900-seat Veterans Memorial Auditorium houses the largest and most acclaimed theatre stage in the state. Home of the Rhode Island Philharmonic and the Festival Ballet, the VMA is proudly situated adjacent to the meticulously restored neoclassical Renaissance Providence Hotel.

BENEFIT STREET
A MILE OF HISTORY

With its brick herringbone sidewalks and lantern-lined streets, Benefit Street boasts one of America's most impressive concentrations of restored colonial homes.

A favorite haunt for authors Edgar Allen Poe and H. P. Lovecraft, the area is also the site of the Nightingale-Brown house, the Old State House, the Licht Judicial Complex, the Providence Athenaeum, the John Brown House Museum and the Museum of the School of Design (RISD).

ELEVATED VIEW OF RISD

Rhode Island School of Design's urban campus lines the Providence River and marks the entry to the city's East Side, where Providence's first residents settled.

RISD is widely perceived as an Ivy League equivalent in art schools. Thanks to RISD and its neighbor, Brown University, Providence claims the largest number of working artists per capita in the nation.

AERIAL VIEW OF WATERFIRE

Crowds line Waterplace Park's tidal basin along the Woonasquatucket River, drawn by the blazing bonfires of Barnaby Evans' WaterFire display. The park has become the center for a variety of cultural events which routinely bring tens of thousands of people into the heart of Providence.

THE OLD CANTEEN
OFFERING ALL THE FLAVORS OF ITALY

Festive and inviting, the glittering sign of Joe Marzilli's Old Canteen evokes the ambiance of a past era.

Established in 1956, this fine Italian restaurant has been a landmark in Providence's Italian neighborhood for over half a century.

AFTER THE RAIN

The focal point of historic Federal Hill, the splashing fountain at DePasquale Square has been romancing locals and tourists for decades.

Here, the fountain awaits the hundreds of people who will pass through its cobblestone piazza on their way to and from dinner at one of Federal Hill's many fine restaurants.

DEPASQUALE FOUNTAIN IN THE SNOW

A snow storm in DePasquale Square: The perfect excuse to seek warmth (and dessert) inside one of Federal Hill's exquisite Italian cafes or renowned bakeries.

SNOWFALL ON FEDERAL HILL

The restaurants lining Atwells Avenue beckon warmly through a heavy New England snowfall. Fine dining and the ambience of a bygone era make Federal Hill a unique destination for anyone who truly appreciates great food.

SNOWFALL AT SLATER MILL

*Pawtucket's Slater Mill, built in 1793, was the nation's first
commercially successful cotton-spinning mill with a fully mechanized power system.*

*It is recognized as the birthplace of the Industrial Revolution in the United States.
Now a National Historic Landmark and museum, the mill hosts a variety of
educational and community events.*

THE VAN WICKLE GATES
Brown University

One of the most recognizable icons of Brown University,
the elegant Van Wickle Gates, donated by alumnus Augustus Van Wickle,
have guarded its main campus area for over a century.

The gates remain closed with the exception of two special occasions each year:
student admission, when they open inward, and commencement day,
when they open outward.

HAVEN BROTHERS

Every day of the year, since 1888,
the Haven Brothers Diner parks in a reserved space beside Providence City Hall,
ready to serve diners into the wee hours of the morning.

THE AVON CINEMA

Located on teeming Thayer Street near Brown University,
the vintage Art Deco style Avon Cinema has been in continuous operation since 1938.

It presently specializes in the exhibition of foreign, independent and documentary films.

MANCHESTER STREET POWER STATION

Glowing like a massive lantern at the edge of the Providence River, Manchester Street Power Station has been in operation since 1903. Easily recognized by its three 321-foot smokestacks, the station is fueled by natural gas and is a vital source of energy for the city.

UP ON THE ROOF
The Biltmore Hotel

The bright red glow of the Providence Biltmore's giant neon letters punctuates the sky as dusk descends over the city of Providence. Considered the grande dame of Providence's historic hotels, the Neo-Federal Beaux-Arts style Biltmore has remained a Rhode Island tradition since 1922.

9

MOONRISE OVER PROVIDENCE

This unique perspective showcases downtown Providence with Kennedy Plaza and the Fleet Skating Center in the foreground, the Bank of America Building in the center, and the glowing red signature of the legendary Biltmore Hotel just right of center.

THE RHODE ISLAND STATEHOUSE
& WATERPLACE PARK BASIN

Prominently situated atop Smith Hill, the Rhode Island Statehouse is topped with a gold-covered bronze statue called the Independent Man.

Created by artist George Brewster in 1899 and crafted by the Gorham Manufacturing Co., the Independent Man stands more than 11 feet tall and weighs more than 500 pounds.

Here, he oversees a crowd gathered for a special event in the tidal basin of Waterplace Park.

NIGHT LIGHTS
PROVIDENCE AT DUSK

The city's lights glow brightly, illuminating the horizon as night falls on Providence.
The sleekly modern, newly constructed I-way bridge complements the historic architecture and bold neon of the Biltmore Hotel, uniting old and new in the constantly evolving city.

THE BANK OF AMERICA BUILDING
VIEW THROUGH THE CLOCKTOWER

Often referred to by locals as the "Superman Building," the 428-foot, 26-floor Bank of America Building has remained the tallest building in Providence since its 1928 completion.

THE PROVIDENCE SKYLINE AT TWILIGHT

Smoke-like pink clouds seem to invade the city just moments after the sun disappears behind the Providence skyline.

THE PROVIDENCE PERFORMING ARTS CENTER

Originally opened in 1928 as Lowe's Movie Palace, the center now hosts Broadway, local, and regional stage performances. P.P.A.C.'S sparkling beauty, combined with the excellence of its productions, make this magnificent theatre a favorite showplace for the arts.

HISTORIC COLLEGE HILL

*Located atop a steep hill rising from the east bank of the Providence River,
the East Side neighborhood of Providence is home to one of the nation's finest collections of architecture
from the late 1700s and early 1800s. At the base of College Hill is the first Baptist Church in America, founded in 1638.*

THE CARRIE BROWN BAJNOTTI MEMORIAL FOUNTAIN

BURNSIDE PARK

This award-winning fountain is a memorial to Caroline Brown (1841-1892) whose husband commissioned it to be sculpted by Enid Yandell. Entitled "The Struggle of Life," the sculpture depicts a winged angel attempting to break free of earthly tendencies.

PASTICHE FINE DESSERTS AND CAFÉ

With its cozy atmosphere and delightful hand-crafted desserts,
Pastiche's intimate European-style café has earned a reputation
as one of the most charming dessert spots in Rhode Island

CRESCENT PARK LOOFF CAROUSEL

Nationally recognized as a masterpiece of wood sculpture,
East Providence's elaborate Crescent Park Carousel was designed in 1895
by Danish immigrant Charles I.D. Looff.

Containing 62 hand-carved figures and an original band organ,
the carousel was adopted by the Rhode Island General Assembly in 1985
as the "State Jewel of American Folk Art."

THE RHODE ISLAND QUARTER

*Since the Ocean State is also known as the "Sailing Capital of the World,"
it is fitting that the 2001 Rhode Island quarter features an image of
a vintage sailboat gliding through Narragansett Bay.*

*The vessel depicted is the famous Herreshoff yacht, RELIANCE,
which won the America's Cup in 1903 and is regarded as
Captain Nat Herreshoff's greatest creation.*

CREATED WITH LOVE
FOR MY SIX BROTHERS AND SISTERS:

BENJAMIN, ROSANNE, GABRIEL
CHRISTOPHER, NICHOLAS AND ISABELLA

CONTRIBUTORS:
ANDY PROEHL – MAP OF PROVIDENCE
DR. PAT CONLEY – HISTORIAN-EDITOR
JOHN BEAUPRÉ – FOREWORD & COPY-EDITOR
BOBBY YAO – RESEARCH
KRISTINE COLE – LAYOUT & GRAPHICS
MICHAEL PAGE – ON PRESS ADVISOR

SPECIAL THANKS TO:
MICHAEL PAGE, BOB SHELLEY, A BIRD'S EYE VIEW HELICOPTERS, DR. PAT CONLEY
AND PRESIDENT BOB NANGLE & V.P. STEPHEN LEE OF MERIDIAN PRINTING

STEPHANIE IZZO DECEMBER 2009

WWW.STEPHANIEIZZO.COM